On My Last Nerve

My Trigeminal Neuralgia and Triumphant
Survival through God's Glory

MONICA CAYCE

WESTBOW
PRESS®
A DIVISION OF THOMAS NELSON
& ZONDERVAN

Scriptures taken from the Holy Bible, New International Version®, NIV®. Copyright © 1973, 1978, 1984, 2011 by Biblica, Inc.™ Used by permission of Zondervan. All rights reserved worldwide. www.zondervan.com The "NIV" and "New International Version" are trademarks registered in the United States Patent and Trademark Office by Biblica, Inc.™

WestBow Press books may be ordered through booksellers or by contacting:

WestBow Press
A Division of Thomas Nelson & Zondervan
1663 Liberty Drive
Bloomington, IN 47403
www.westbowpress.com
1 (866) 928-1240

Library of Congress Control Number: 2017917296
ISBN: 978-1-9736-0744-1 (sc)
ISBN: 978-1-9736-0743-4 (e)

Print information available on the last page.

WestBow Press rev. date: 11/21/2017

I dedicate this book to my sister, Tammy, who never left my side. Without her love and care, my outcome would have been different. We all share the same God, but I wish everyone had a sister like her.

To my children and grandchildren: My greatest comfort is to know that this condition is not hereditary and that I cannot pass this down to any of you in the future. My wish for all of you is that you walk with Christ and have joy. Remember to smile for all the times that I couldn't.

Whatever you do whether in word or deed, do it all in the name of The Lord Jesus, giving thanks to God the Father through him. (Colossians 3:17)

My favorite Bible verse is Psalm 46:10: "Be still and know that I am God."

A similar Bible verse is found in Exodus 14:14: "The Lord will fight for you; you only need to be still."

Contents

Preface

I experienced frustration, aggravation, torment, and fighting something I did not quite understand. For years, I suffered in pain and was aggravated with others and myself. Was I going crazy? Even the sound of the television hurt the inside of my head.

I had occurrences of extremely high blood pressure. My head kept hurting. I had continuous dental interventions because my teeth hurt. I had extensive eye evaluations because my eye hurt. What was happening to me? I was literally on my last nerve with everyone including myself.

This book is my journey from a misdiagnosis to a correct one. I suffered through one of the worst pains known to mankind—*trigeminal neuralgia*. These are two big words, but there are two that are much bigger—*Jesus Christ*.

I wrote this book to bring about the much-needed awareness of trigeminal neuralgia. This is not a self-help book. It is a God help book. I pray your mind and heart will be open while reading my book.

—Monica Cayce

Chapter 1

Trigeminal Neuralgia

Facts about Trigeminal Neuralgia

1. Trigeminal neuralgia (TN) is regarded as the most painful medical condition.
2. My neurosurgeon explained that trigeminal neuralgia is believed to go back as far as the days when pirates sailed the seas.
3. TN is also called the suicide syndrome. If you have had a family member who committed suicide by drug overdose, please read my book.
4. Most research on TN describes the facial pain that is experienced as short jabs lasting seconds to a few minutes. My facial spasms lasted thirty minutes and sometimes hours. There wasn't anything short about my pain.
5. TN is usually present years before it's diagnosed. Early diagnosis can prevent more nerve damage.

What Is Trigeminal Neuralgia?

The trigeminal nerve is the fifth cranial nerve. The nerve originates in the brain stem and runs along both sides of the face. It is called the trigeminal nerve because it has three branches, which control sensations in the upper, middle, and lower portions of the face.

There are two forms of TN. The typical form or type 1 causes a sudden, burning, shock-like, facial pain. The atypical form or type 2 causes a constant aching, burning, and stabbing pain.

This condition affects one side of the face. Rarely are both sides affected at the same time.

What Causes Trigeminal Neuralgia?

A myelin sheath surrounds the trigeminal nerve and serves as a protective coating (like the coating around an extension cord). The cerebral artery beats against this myelin sheath and, over time, causes its protective coating to wear away (demyelination). This causes the cerebral artery to have direct contact with the nerve, creating neuropathic facial pain on that side of the face. The pain is similar to a dentist touching a nerve while drilling on a tooth.

There are many suspected causes of trigeminal neuralgia. I believe my cause was related to my previous brain tumor.

It is reported that one in fifteen thousand people suffer from this disease. I think the number is much higher because the condition is often misdiagnosed as a dental problem and even mental illness. The disease is usually diagnosed in middle age but can be seen in patients as young as three years old.

Chapter 2

When God Wants Something

I never had a desire to write a book. I never knew how. I have a full-time nursing job. But God's plan was for me to write this book. I did not hear His voice. I just felt His Spirit of direction.

After my surgery, I was at a follow-up visit with my neurologist. I told him that there wasn't enough public awareness about trigeminal neuralgia and that someone from the Acadian area where I live, should write a book about the disease.

"You do it and title the book *On My Nerve*," he said.

I laughed and said, "Yeah, *On My Last Nerve*."

Was that God's way of speaking to me? It got me thinking about writing a book on TN, and I discussed it with my neurosurgeon.

He said, "Do it."

Was that God's way of speaking to me again? At that time, I was going through a divorce.

I told my surgeon, "But I'm so angry right now. I'm scared I will write about angry things."

"It's your story," he said.

I did not know how to write a book. God directed me to go to school where I could learn how to do it.

But I would tell myself, *Don't be silly. You work a daytime shift as a nurse.* I worked at a cardiology clinic for twenty years. I had never had the option to work anything but the day shift in the clinic. Miraculously around this time, a night shift was created and offered to me. I took the position, which allowed me to go to a writing class during the daytime.

Writing a book was now part of my plans. I realized that God was using me to get His message to His children. But what was the message? Was it just trigeminal neuralgia awareness? I struggled to understand what message God wanted me to carry out.

I was praying one morning for God to show me His wisdom and direction. His Spirit overwhelmed me with this answer: *Tell people about me! Tell them everything that you conquered was all in my glory!*

I am a God-fearing woman. I did not want to write about my *glory story* because it is God's *glory story*. He is our Lord of lords and King of kings.

I knew then that I would write a book and the reason I must write it. But there were financial hurdles to get over. It costs money to write and publish a book. I was a single woman paying all my bills by myself, with no spousal support. But I couldn't forget whose plan this was.

One day I went to the mailbox and received a large, unexpected check. I had overpaid while the house I had just sold was in escrow. I smiled and said to God, *Okay, we got this now!*

Later while drinking coffee with my writing instructor, I asked, "Why would God choose me to write a book? My sister is the avid reader in our family. Her vocabulary surpasses mine."

My instructor said, "But you have the story."

For I know the plans I have for you, declares the Lord, plans to prosper you and not harm you, plans to give you hope and a future. (Jeremiah 29:11)

Chapter 3

The Beginning

Where do I start? Let's start at the beginning of my path and not my life. I feel that my life did not start until I was on God's path.

I lived in a small country town. When I was young, I had been embarrassed to tell anyone where I lived. The layout of the town was pretty simple: two schools, two stores, four churches, two fire departments, and no traffic lights.

As an adult, I became proud of my hometown. I would defend its honor. It later became the resting place of the people I had known as a child. The town had four graveyards.

In my small hometown, there were three denominations a person could practice or follow. You could be a Catholic, a Baptist, or a Methodist. I was raised in the Catholic church. I also raised both of my children to be Catholics.

When my children became adults, I started searching for another church. I felt that I needed something different in my life—a better relationship with Christ. So after seeking out many different churches, one Sunday morning, I walked into the Gibson Baptist Church. I can't explain the love that was driven inside me that day. I felt like my heart found a home.

When I was a baby, I had been baptized in the Catholic church.

The belief had been that baptism had washed away the original sin I had been born with. Now I decided to be baptized again in the Baptist church because the first baptism was my parents' decision but this one was mine. I accepted Jesus Christ as my Lord and Savior, and I wanted to start living for Him instead of myself.

After that, the devil got mad. Mind-blowing things happened in my life. My boyfriend and I had a terrible breakup. Then after agreeing to travel to New Orleans to see if we could reconcile the relationship, I had a syncopal (fainting) episode there.

My belly was full of raw oysters from the Acme Oyster House. We were listening to a rock-in-roll band at a place called "The Famous Door". I fell forward without anything breaking my fall and hit the right side of my face on the red brick floor. My head actually bounced off the floor and hit it a second time. I ended up with two large knots on my right temple.

It's hard for me to articulate my brief experience during my fall, but it was definitely an unforgettable experience. It was very dark. I felt weightless. There was a cool, silent atmosphere. I heard angelic music in the distance—no instruments, just female-like voices that sang beautiful, flowing music. I felt confused in that place and forgot about it the moment I opened my eyes. It seemed like I'd just blinked.

When I opened my eyes, my boyfriend's face was right there. He asked, "Are you okay?"

I thought, *What a silly question*, so I returned his question. Then wow! Boy did I feel pain. It felt like someone had hit the side of my head with a baseball bat. I asked him if someone had hit me. He told me that I had fallen.

I looked at him in disbelief and asked, "I fell?" He had obviously picked me up because I was now standing as I had been before the fall. This made it hard for me to understand that I *had* fallen. My head was throbbing to the point of nausea.

He asked, "Can you walk?"

I answered, "I think so."

We walked out together, and no one else came to my aid or asked if I needed any help. Were they used to seeing this in New Orleans?

My head felt like it was spinning. My boyfriend wanted to take me to the hospital, but this took place in January 2007, right after Hurricane Katrina had devastated the area. Because I was a nurse, I knew that many medical personnel had left the area, so I refused to go. I told him that I wanted to wait until I could go to a hospital close to my home. I wanted to see my own doctor. Waiting to seek medical care had not been a wise decision. I might have had a fatal head injury.

After I returned home, I had a CAT scan at the clinic where I worked. It revealed a five-millimeter calcium deposit in the fourth ventricle of my brain. I took those results to a neurologist I used to work for. He ordered an MRI, which showed more of the tumor.

Its size was actually three and a half centimeters, which was the size of a large olive. It was right on top of my brain stem. That's not a good place to have a brain tumor, but when God's in charge, it doesn't matter where it is.

Both my daughter and my son's girlfriend were pregnant at that time. I remember asking my neurologist, "Will I get to see any of my grandchildren?" He smiled and reassured me that I would. To bring you up to date, I now have seven grandchildren.

Be joyful, in hope, patient in affliction, faithful in Prayer. (Romans 12:12)

Chapter 4

Surgery to Remove My Brain Tumor

I believe that nothing happens by accident. I feel everything happens for a purpose and is in God's plan.

My neurologist called and asked me whom I wanted as my surgeon. He told me that the MRI results didn't seem to show that I had like a malignant tumor, but it was so close to the brain stem, it would have to be removed. Of course, I named the best neurosurgeon in Thibodaux. He said he would arrange it for me.

When I got to my surgeon's office, I signed my name under his on the check-in sheet and sat down. Then the nurse called my name and brought me to the back. She asked me several questions and before she left the room, she mentioned that a different neurosurgeon would be right in. I immediately said, "Wait, that isn't who I'm seeing. I'm seeing the doctor that I requested."

She came back into the room and explained that this surgeon had taught the one that I had requested. I thought on that for a few minutes and answered, "Well, I guess this is what God wants, so I'll meet him." He was supposed to be a wonderful surgeon, and besides, the one I had originally requested would be assisting him in my surgery. I couldn't ask for anything better.

Before they brought me into surgery to shave my head, I wanted to see my preacher. He asked me, "Jo, if you don't make it through this surgery, do you believe without a shadow of a doubt, will you go to heaven?"

I thought about that and answered, "Well, I didn't kill anyone; I think I'm a good person."

He repeated the same question to me again. I told him, "Yes," but was I really sure?

I repeated what my preacher had asked when my sister came in to see me. She told me, "It's not what you did or didn't do. It's what Jesus did. He paid for your salvation." At that moment, I thought, *It all makes sense now.*

The surgeon performed a posterior craniotomy to remove my brain tumor. It was done on February 13, 2007. The surgery was supposed to take three hours but only took one.

The surgeon reported a successful outcome for my surgery. The roots from the tumor did not grow towards the brain stem, so he was able to remove all the tumor and its roots. God is so good!

I stayed in ICU for three days and went into a regular room for two more days before going home. I asked to have something for the pain in ICU. I was told that I couldn't have anything for pain because it would mask intracranial pressure symptoms. The medications I received in the hospital were codeine injections that made me go to sleep. When I woke up, my head hurt so bad, but God got me through it all.

My tumor was diagnosed as a choroid plexus papilloma—a benign tumor located within the brain's ventricles from the cells in the choroid plexus. My tumor was located in the fourth ventricle of my brain.

My mother took care of me when I went home. She was a good nurse. I was back working as a full-time nurse eight weeks later.

For it is by grace you have been saved, through faith and this not from yourselves, it is the gift of God not by works, so that no one can boast. (Ephesians 2:8)

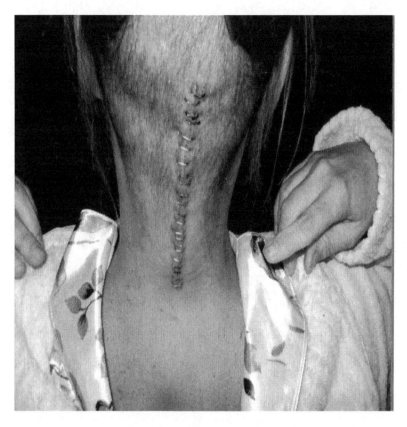

3 Days After My Posterior Craniectomy 2-15-07

Chapter 5

Signs, Symptoms, and Diagnosis of Trigeminal Neuralgia

Approximately two years before I was diagnosed with TN, my wisdom tooth on the lower left side of my jaw started hurting. I went to a dentist in Houma. He performed a root canal on that tooth. The tooth was still hurting a week after the procedure.

I called my dentist's office, and he told me I probably had an infection at the root canal site. He prescribed a strong antibiotic, which I completed, but the area continued to hurt. I called back a couple of weeks later to report that I was still in pain. He examined the root canal in his office and explained that it appeared to be fine and would just need a little time for the pain to subside.

I didn't understand that explanation. I had had a root canal on the other side of my mouth, but it hadn't continued to hurt like this. I didn't want to be a bad patient, so I gave it a few more weeks. However, my jaw pain never ceased. I made another trip back to his office, and again, he had no explanation as to why the area was still hurting.

Weeks turned into months. I moved two hours away from where I had been living to Lafayette. The Acadian area is beautiful with the friendliest people. I settled in my new home and workplace. Like everyone who moves, I had to find new doctors and dentists. I had to wait two months before I could get an appointment as a new patient.

I started having pain in my left eye. The pain felt similar to someone pushing on my eye. At first, I thought I had dry eye because my new job position required that I look at a computer screen for long periods of time to code and bill office visits and diagnostic testing. I bought eye drops, which were ineffective.

My grandmother had had glaucoma, so I decided to see an ophthalmologist. My eye evaluation even involved some neurologic testing because of my brain tumor history. All tests were negative, but I was diagnosed with stage 1 cataracts. The cataract patients I knew never complained of pain, but in nursing, I learned to never say never.

I was also unaware that my eye was hurting on the same side of my head as my tooth. It took me a few months before I could get to see a new dentist. They took X-rays, and then I waited there two hours before the new dentist came into my room.

He told me to go back to the dentist in Houma that had performed my root canal. Really? I could have driven to Houma in the two hours I had to wait for him to tell me that. But he did refer me to a root canal specialist.

The specialist took more X-rays and reported that he didn't see anything wrong. He could try to fix it but might have to refer me to an oral surgeon to pull it anyway. I thanked him but decided that I had spent enough time and money on that tooth for him to try to fix it.

I went to the oral surgeon the specialist had recommended and had him pull the tooth. At last, it was gone! However, the tooth was gone but not the pain. I waited months for it to heal. My bottom jaw still hurt. For some reason, the pain was worst at night.

I went to another dentist my coworker recommended—a local one in Lafayette. I explained that I thought the surgeon had pulled the wrong tooth. I told him that it must be the tooth next to the one that was pulled, because my jaw was still hurting.

He took more X-rays and explained that he didn't see anything wrong with the tooth. I had had enough of that terrible pain. I had been fighting with that jaw pain for almost two years now and was very frustrated. I asked him very sternly, "Who is going to pull this tooth, you or me?"

So, he pulled it because I insisted. I gave the jaw a few weeks to heal, but the pain remained. I went back to the dentist and reported how the pain was still there. He made me point to the location of the pain. I did, and he explained how there was no tooth there. He was right. Was I crazy?

He had a sad expression as he said, "I think you may have trigeminal neuralgia." I had heard of that before but didn't know much about it. He explained how the trigeminal nerve ran alongside my jawline, exactly where I was hurting.

I asked him if he could just cut the nerve out. His assistant brought in a model of the human skull so he could educate me. He said that there were small openings, one on each side of the bottom jaw, where bundles of nerves came out. The hole on the left side of the jaw was exactly where I was hurting. It was a textbook case!

He referred me to a neurologist of my choosing. I think as soon as my brain heard the diagnosis, all the symptoms came forth with a vengeance. But I will always remember and be grateful to Dentist Carl Breaux, my hero!

I had another dental appointment a year after my MVD (micro vascular decompression) surgery. I asked Dentist Breaux his permission to take a picture of him and tell the events that led him to diagnose me with TN. He agreed to be included in my book. He also revealed to me that his father-in-law had trigeminal neuralgia and that's why he thought I had it. Thank you, Jesus, for placing me in the presence of your angels and blessing my life.

Dentist Carl Breaux (My Hero) and Monica Cayce

Chapter 6

The Month I Was Dying

This was the most difficult chapter for me to write. It is my journey into the torments of hell. I don't like thinking about that place. I pray and thank God daily for bringing me out of that dark, painful world. My wish is that everyone would become aware that there is hope and help in Jesus Christ. If you are in a state of affliction, all you have to do is ask Jesus to come into your life. It's that easy. Accept Him as your Lord and Savior. He is waiting for you to admit that you need Him.

It was the beginning of September 2013, when I first saw my neurologist. He confirmed, by my symptoms alone, that I definitely had TN but scheduled an MRI for me anyway. He asked if I needed a prescription for pain medication. I declined because narcotics make me nauseated and constipated, which just wasn't worth it at that point. I thought that if I had to live with TN, I would have to deal with the pain. I didn't want to be dependent on narcotics. As a nurse, I have seen narcotics ruin too many lives. He did prescribe seventy-five milligrams of Lyrica to help with the pain. It was to be taken twice a day. I thought that I could manage my pain with Advil. Boy, was I ever wrong!

Your brain has a protective mechanism that suppresses

memories of horrific events you experience. It has been over two years since I went through that time in my life. I have allowed myself to forget that tragic, painful period.

Because I was a nurse, my documenting skills took over during that time. The following details are actual notes, which I wrote down on small pieces of paper and in a composition book. They bring back those painful memories I have forgotten.

One personality trait that every nurse possesses is the desire to help people. I believe at that time, I didn't think that I was going to survive TN, so I must have documented my experiences in hopes of helping others. When I write about a spasm, it means I experienced the same feeling as when a dentist hits a nerve while drilling in the mouth. It was a burning, shocking feeling.

My Notes

September 3, 2013

One hour of sleep. Left upper and lower jaw pain. Left head pain. Took Advil and Lyrica. Top teeth on left side pulsating pain. Hurt all night.

September 4, 2013

One hour of sleep. Left upper and lower jaw pain. Feels like my left upper teeth have hot rocks being nailed through them. Left head pain. Took Advil and extra Lyrica. Didn't help with the pain. Hurt all night.

September 5, 2013

Left upper and lower jaw pain. Left ear pain. Feels like a hot nail is being inserted into my eardrum. Left head pain. Called neurologist today for the prescription of pain meds that he had previously offered.

At this point of my suffering, I had changed my mind and needed the medication. His nurse had to ask him before she could send narcotics to the pharmacy.

I took Advil, Tylenol, two Lyrica, and two old Percocets that I had left over from a previous surgery. I just got nauseated and received no relief from the pain. Fell asleep at 4:00 a.m.

September 6, 2013

Had a thirty-minute facial spasm after eating ice cream. Had to call my neurologist office again to ask his nurse to please ask my doctor for the pain meds. It made me feel like a drug seeker. I received a prescription that day for Lortab. Slept in my bed for the first time in four nights.

September 8, 2013

7:00 p.m. to midnight had no relief from meds. Had twelve spasms. Hot pain from left top cheek to left eye. I could hear the static-popping current traveling down the nerve path in my head. It is so hot and it burns.

September 9, 2013

For some reason, when laying down flat it would cause a spasm. I think the artery would compress on the nerve at that position. My MRI was scheduled today. I took an old valium and was able to lie down in the machine and complete the test.

Had to go to the ER in Lafayette after MRI test was completed. Was in the ER for six hours. No one could see the pain in my head. I asked to be admitted for pain management. I had not slept in two weeks, and my body was exhausted. Was told I couldn't be admitted for TN and there was no pain management in that hospital.

The NP in the ER reviewed my MRI that I had just completed and reported the results were normal. Received a Dilaudid injection with Phenergan with a prescription for Dilaudid to take home. I was discharged with an appointment to see my neurologist the next day. Slept that night for the first time in two weeks.

September 10, 2013

Took Dilaudid oral medication before going to neurologist appointment. I felt so drowsy, my husband had to drive me there.

My neurologist calls the neurosurgeon while in the room with me to see if he could refer me there for gamma knife evaluation. I had explained to him that I was scheduled to go with my church to Haiti on a mission trip at the beginning of October. To my surprise, the neurosurgeon told me to come right over to see him. That was a miracle within itself, because it usually takes three months to get an appointment there.

The same MRI of my brain that was reported as normal in the hospital ER was now on the neurosurgeon's computer. He pointed to the exact spot on my trigeminal nerve that was being compressed by an artery. He also explained that the gamma knife procedure was not an option for me. In his opinion, I needed a brain surgery called MVD (micro vascular decompression).

An incision would be made behind my left ear. My occipital bone would be removed to expose the protective covering of my brain called the dura. The dura would then be cut open to expose my brain. He would then go into my brain and wrap a Teflon sponge around my trigeminal nerve to prevent contact from the artery causing the shocking spasms that I was having.

He explained that he would be going out of the country on a trip for a few weeks, but his partner could perform the procedure. I decided to try and wait for him to come back. That also meant my mission trip to Haiti would have to be cancelled for me. My misfortune was someone else's blessing. It allowed a college student to go in my place.

I believe everything happens in God's time. The neurosurgeon gave me the best prescription that day to treat my TN. He prescribed Tegretal 200mg, and I could take it four times a day. I was also given a prescription for a steroid dose pack.

September 11, 2013

Was kind of a blur. Was taking the steroids and Tegretal four times daily; Advil, Lyrica twice daily; Lortabs, Dilaudids, and Phenergan. I was over medicated.

September 12–13, 2013

Stayed sitting up in the bed. Couldn't lie down because spasms would immediately occur. I was starting to lose my vision and also lose my thought process. I was becoming zombie-like. I couldn't read, and I couldn't remember my Bible verses. I was afraid the devil was trying to steal my mind. But for some reason I could still sing songs in my mind—songs that brought love in my heart. The devil was no match for love. It keeps him away. I can remember singing "Victory in Jesus" in my mind.

September 14–15, 2013

I could just lay in the bed now. I felt so lethargic. I couldn't get out of bed. I brought all my medication to bed with me. I don't remember eating or drinking. Was in the bedroom on the other side of the house so I wouldn't disturb my husband. I think he was quite aggravated with me by this point. I don't think he understood that I needed a calm quiet atmosphere. I went to seek comfort in the bedroom that had a window valance with the Bible verse, Psalm 1:18. I will both lie down in peace and sleep, for you alone, Oh Lord, make me dwell in safety.

September 16, 2013

My sister came and found me in the bed like a zombie. She gave me water and left to go get me some soup to eat. She came back and fed me. She is also a nurse and recognized that I was over medicated at that point. She told me to decrease my Tegretal and Lyrica. I did decrease my Tegretal to three times daily and discontinued my Lortabs. And then things started improving.

September 17, 2013

I wasn't lethargic anymore. My vision was returning. I was able to have a thought process again. I decided at that point to start documenting a MAR (medication administration record) to prevent an accidental drug overdose.

I realized now why TN is also called the suicide syndrome. It is my opinion the people diagnosed with TN that committed suicide actually didn't want to kill themselves. I believe their thought process was taken away, and they accidentally took an overdose of their medications. If I wasn't a nurse with documenting skills, I would have never found my therapeutic medication levels. I believe my outcome would have been different had my sister not stopped by that day.

The key to this condition is a quiet, calm, and loving atmosphere. Controlling your blood pressure and taking anti-inflammatory medication with Tegretal was my best regimen. Early diagnosis is the utmost importance to prevent more damage to the myelin sheath around the trigeminal nerve.

It didn't take me long to figure out what caused my spasms. I stopped chewing, stopped drinking cold or hot liquids, stopped brushing my teeth on the left side of my mouth, stopped wearing makeup, and turned off ceiling fans. I couldn't smile. I lost thirty pounds in one month.

When I would have a spasm, I would grab the left side of my head with my left hand and I would raise my right hand in the air to hold Jesus' hand. If I was standing by the time the spasm was over, I was down on my knee. But I was still holding on the Jesus's hand. He never let go. Love will always help you through your pain

For I am the Lord your God who takes hold of your right hand and says to you, Do Not Fear; I will help you. (Isaiah 41:13)

Holding Jesus' Hand During a TN Spasm

Chapter 7

My MVD Surgery

I tried to wait until the neurosurgeon, whom I had met, came back from his trip out of the country to perform my surgery, but my spasms became more frequent. My body became weaker, and I decided to meet with his partner to schedule the MVD surgery.

I was quite impressed with the second neurosurgeon. He was such a humble doctor. My heart was convinced that he was the surgeon for me. I felt God leading me on this path and followed. I couldn't lose with this decision. If I didn't survive the surgery, I would run right into the arms of Jesus, who would be waiting to take me to our Father.

My surgery was scheduled for September 25, 2013—the day before my daughter's birthday. The facial spasms and sleep deprivation went on for a month more. By the end of that month, I was dying. I can't imagine living for years in that condition.

My greatest wish for everyone is that you are living with someone who loves you. It is absolutely awful when you are sick and dying to have to argue with others. That is the time in your life when you will need love, support, and understanding.

My son drove in from Alabama the night before my surgery. He drove me to the hospital the next morning. I had to be at the hospital at 5:00 a.m. I checked into the hospital and sat in the waiting area until they called my name.

My sister walked into the lobby and saw me holding my head. She asked, "Is your head hurting?"

I answered, "Yes, really bad."

When they called me to the back, it was apparent why my head was hurting. My blood pressure was extremely high. It was too high to proceed with the surgery. I had to receive medicine to lower my blood pressure. My daughter arrived at the hospital around this time.

The surgery team was kind enough to wait until I was under anesthesia before shaving my head. My surgery was supposed to take two hours, but it took four hours to complete. I had a lot of scar tissue and damage on my trigeminal nerve. They had to wrap three sponges around it instead of one.

My first memory in recovery was of seeing my two children. Thank you, Jesus! God is so good! Then my sister came in. She asked if she could do anything for me. I asked her to sing "Victory in Jesus." Recently, she told me the nurse who hooked me up to the monitors looked at her to see if she would start singing, and of course, she swallowed her pride and answered her sister's request.

My chest and head hurt so bad. Because I'm a cardiovascular nurse, the first thing I thought was, *I'm having a heart attack*. I wanted the nurse to get the doctor I worked for at the heart clinic. I started calling out his name. The nurse asked my sister why I was calling his name, to which she responded, "I have no idea." Thinking about it now, it seems so funny. But it sure wasn't funny then.

My preacher and his wife came in and prayed for me. I barely remember my sister-in-law and a coworker visiting. I was on some major pain medication, unlike the first brain surgery.

I saw black rats running across the floor that night. Then I heard the pain pump on my left side call out my name. I thought to myself, *You are hallucinating. Don't look at it. Keep looking straight ahead.* Then, it called out my name again. I slowly turned my head to the left and looked at it. It didn't look any different. It was the same old pain pump. But then it said, "God's blood's good."

I called out to my sister, who was sleeping on the side of my bed. She woke up and asked, "What?" in her sleepiness. I told her what the pain pump said. She said in a calm voice, "It is. Now go back to sleep." She went back to sleep because she had to go to work at another hospital the next morning (My sister is also a nurse). I never hallucinated again after that night.

I had nausea and vomiting for three days. I lost ten pounds in three days. The second day, I lost my hearing in my left ear. After they removed a paper bowl, which had been taped to the left side of my head to prevent any contact with my incision, I realized that I couldn't hear out of that ear. Then when I sat in a chair, my nose started to bleed. After that, I could hear out of my left ear again. I had had a difficult time getting off oxygen. After another nosebleed, it seemed that I could breathe better. Then I didn't need the oxygen.

The nurse came in my room with a cup of ice. She wanted me to chew on the ice, to see if I would get a facial spasm. I was so scared and didn't want to chew it. With her encouragement, I did. There was no spasm that happened. YEAH! The surgery proved to be successful!

I remember my mom and stepdad's visit in the ICU. My mom kept asking me questions, and I couldn't talk because it hurt my head too much. Thank God for modern technology. I discovered texting was my way to communicate with everyone.

My sister stayed with me and even slept with me when I got home. She was my sense of comfort. She had to leave the next day to go on the Haiti mission with our church members.

I remember taking a shower the next morning at home. It felt so good to have the hot water run down my back, but I felt weak when I saw the blood and flesh, which had been connected to my hair, hit the shower floor. I got dressed but then had to go lay down.

My preacher and his son came to visit me at home. My husband told him, "Can you believe that she is a nurse and got weak seeing some blood and hair in the shower?"

My preacher responded, "Yes, I imagine it's difficult when it's your own blood and hair."

Good answer, I thought. My preacher told me that I looked much better. I said, "Thank you." Little comments like that mean so much when you feel bad and so ugly.

I would like to thank the wonderful company I'm employed with. I was off work for one month before my surgery and three months after it. My job was waiting for me when I returned. Thanks to all of my coworkers for picking up my slack while I was out.

It wasn't long before I discovered that my sense of taste was gone. The only types of food that I could taste were sweets. Before the surgery, I never craved sweets. Now that had all changed. However, I could start chewing and eating again.

Loud sounds still hurt my head. I felt like I missed the bonding experience with my daughter's third baby. When the baby cried, I had to get away from the sound. It hurt my head so bad. My daughter stayed away from me most of the time because it was too painful for me. It took about a year before I could tolerate the loud volume of a movie theater.

This is actually the second time I have written this book. After my MVD surgery, I became legally separated from my husband and filed for a divorce. I had written a few chapters on the ugly details. I had wanted everyone to know that even if you are mentally and physically defeated, God could pull you out of it all because there is victory in Jesus.

After I had turned the first manuscript into my publisher, my heart had not been at peace with it. I had known that God didn't want me to include all that mess. I had been afraid that my book would not get God's blessing if I had defied His wishes. After months of thinking and praying for wisdom and direction from God, I took back my first manuscript and deleted some original chapters. However, I will include a few things in hopes that it will help someone else.

I wasn't released to drive after my surgery and needed to get some food. I was so embarrassed and ashamed that I was going through a divorce, I didn't ask for help. I ate eggs for weeks. I kept telling everyone at church that my husband was at the hunting camp. I even told my mom the same story when she came over to visit me. That went on for about three months. Finally, in my Sunday Bible class at church, I announced to everyone that I was getting a divorce. They were all shocked but loved me as family members should.

I became so angry and depressed during this period. My sister would call to check on me, and I would tell her that I was on my knees again. I was on my knees praying because I was so angry with my husband. All that anger was unhealthy for my physical and spiritual well-being. Anger consumed me. I couldn't eat or sleep. I had to lay all that anger down and ask Jesus to please take it away from me. He took it out of my heart.

No one but God carried me through those months. I ran right into his arms for comfort and healing. My weakness faded in His presence. He gave me everlasting strength to survive. Hope in Him protected me from self-pity and pulled me out of my depression. But I had to open my heart and mind and allow Him to bless me with His peace. I couldn't be ashamed of my life and the feelings of emptiness I possessed. Thankful prayers kept my focus on His presence and His promises.

His presence is my companion each step of my journey through life. I keep my eyes focused on Jesus. I trust Him to guide my path and to lead me through any storm that may come.

Yes, I had survived one of the most painful conditions known to mankind and went through a divorce. But I made it through God's glory and the surgery ended all my TN suffering.

> I have told you these things, so that in me you may have peace. In this world, you will have trouble. But take heart! I have overcome the world. (John 16:33)

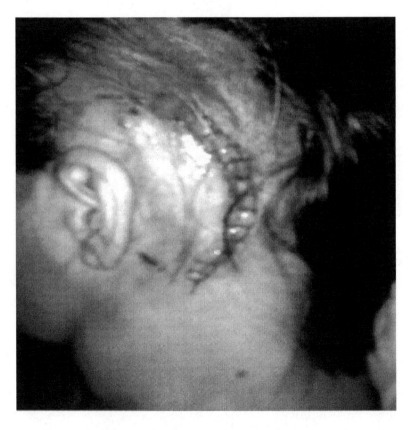

2 Days After My MVD Surgery 9-27-13

Chapter 8

Five Encounters

I had decided after my MVD surgery that if I ever met anyone with TN, I would give that person a compassionate hug and say a prayer for him or her. But of course, things never happen as planned.

I was at my gynecologist's office almost a year after my surgery. I had undressed and was lying on the exam room table in the stirrups for my yearly Pap test. I could hear my doctor talking to his nurse outside my door. I assumed they were discussing details about my medical history.

My doctor entered the room in disbelief and explained that he thought the woman he had just examined had trigeminal neuralgia. He asked if it would be all right if she came in and talked to me about it. He had been explaining to his nurse that he usually only saw someone with TN about every five years and how remarkable it was to have two women in rooms next to each other who had it.

I had learned that nothing happens by accident. I told him that I would talk to her, and in she walked while I was still naked on the exam table. That was my first encounter of meeting someone else with TN. At that point, the hug that I had planned was too awkward.

It didn't take long for the story of my TN journey to spread. I began getting calls and emails with questions about TN. My goal in life became educating not only patients but also their family members and health-care providers.

I thought I would write about the first five people with TN who approached me. Then I decided to let them tell their own stories. I asked each person the same five questions. Their names are not given so as to respect their privacy.

First Encounter

Question: What was your first sign or symptom of TN?

Answer: I had tingling and numbness on the right side of my tongue. Gradually, the numbness went into my palate.

Question: How long did you have these signs or symptoms before you were diagnosed with TN? Answer: One year. I went to gynecologist because she thought they were symptoms of menopause. Then, I went to an ENT, that referred me to a neurologist. I saw two different neurologists. Finally, I was diagnosed with TN.

Question: Was an intervention done before you were diagnosed?

Answer: Yes, a tooth was pulled, and then the numbness started months later.

Question: What intervention was done after you were diagnosed?

Answer: None, I was just medically treated. The symptoms were not bad enough yet.

Question: Where are you right now in regards to your condition?

Answer: No medicine really helps me. Both upper and lower lips are numb now. The entire upper palate and the right side of my tongue are numb all the time, but there is no pain.

Question: What would you like people to know?

Answer: I have been having these symptoms for five years now. The numbness never leaves me. It's something that I just have to accept, live with, and pray it doesn't get worse.

Second Encounter

My second encounter was actually with a coworker. Her brother-in-law was diagnosed with multiple sclerosis (MS) twenty years ago. He has TN because of the MS. He wanted to know who my neurosurgeon was. He ended up being a non-operable patient, but I still wanted to interview him. I thought it might provide someone who has MS with a direction for care.

Question: What was your first sign or symptom of TN?

Answer: Pain when lightly touching my left cheek or turning my head when talking. Chewing also caused pain.

Question: How long did you have these signs or symptoms before you were diagnosed?

Answer: Three months. Kept going to see the doctor about a medicine called Lyrica, which I had seen on a TV commercial.

Question: What intervention was done before you were diagnosed?

Answer: The gamma knife. The first time I had relief for a year and a half. The second time I had no relief at all.

Question: Where are you right now in regards to your condition?

Answer: TN still comes and goes. Nothing specific makes it occur. The medicine Oxycarmazepine helps an hour after taking it.

Question: What would you like people to know?

Answer: Be aware of what triggers the pain. Cold weather and moving my head to the right can trigger my pain.

Third Encounter

My third encounter was with my daughter. She was gathering information for her sister-in-law's father. He also wanted to know the name of my neurosurgeon. This man had a successful surgery and is back to living a normal life.

Question: What was your first sign or symptom of TN?

Answer: A sharp pain in his upper left side of my jaw in the teeth area, which was triggered by chewing, laughing, or just the wind blowing on my face. I would also get a twitch, which would cause the left side of my face to become numb and lasted a few minutes. It was comparable to a large brain freeze, as it temporarily paralyzed me from moving anything so as not to upset the condition until it subsided.

Question: How long did you have these signs or symptoms before you were diagnosed with TN?

Answer: About ten years before being diagnosed by my primary care physician.

Question: What intervention was done before you were diagnosed?

Answer: I took six to eight Motrins a day and had eleven root canals.

Question: What intervention was done after you were diagnosed?

Answer: I was treated with a medication called Gabapentin. A neurologist administered injections around the trigeminal nerve in my face, which would relieve the pain for four to six months. Then more medication and injections were needed. Everything was just a temporary fix. I sought the advice of a friend's father and was evaluated by a neurosurgeon for the cyber gamma knife. But the neurosurgeon recommended the MVD surgery instead. I had the MVD surgery.

Question: Where are you right now in regards to your TN?

Answer: No more pain. No more medicine. All the suffering is gone. I surrendered and gave himself to God. I am truly blessed.

Question: What would you like people to know?

Answer: There are treatments for TN. If you have a chance to do the surgery, please get it done. Don't wait eleven years like me, just treating the symptoms. I want you to have faith in God.

Fourth Encounter

I couldn't interview my fourth person because she is currently receiving psychiatric counseling. I do not know her personally. Another coworker contacted me to get help for this person who was diagnosed with TN.

Anyone who has TN knows that this is a very possible outcome. I remember being in so much pain, I became depressed. I was on so much medicine, I was a zombie at one point. It would have been very easy to just slip away to a darker place. The answer to my victory was Jesus Christ our Lord and Savior. I slept hugging my Bible. His Word was my weapon. God brought me to victory, and He can do the same for anyone.

Fifth Encounter

My fifth encounter was a patient where I work. I was trying to talk to her on the phone one day, and I could not understand her slurred speech. I finally understood she was saying that she had TN. I told her that I knew what she was going through because I had had TN and the MVD surgery. She wanted to know the name of my neurosurgeon. She went to see him and also had the MVD surgery.

Question: What was your first sign or symptom of TN?

Answer: A toothache for one month. I was sent to an oral surgeon who pulled the tooth. I still had the pain, so I went to an internist who referred me to a neurologist.

Question: How long did you have these signs or symptoms before you were diagnosed with TN?

Answer: About two and a half years.

Question: What intervention was done before you were diagnosed?

Answer: A root canal, then would pull the tooth.

Question: What intervention was done after you were diagnosed?

Answer: A neurosurgeon performed the cyber gamma knife procedure, which irritated my TN even more. Then I went to a different neurosurgeon, who performed the MVD surgery. Three weeks after the surgery while getting my sutures removed, there was fluid oozing out of the incision. I was in a lot of pain. Four weeks after my MVD surgery, I had to go back into surgery so they could clean out the infection in my brain.

Question: Where are you right now in regards to your condition?

Answer: I sleep better now but still have pain. I am now getting pain management sessions. My left eye does not close or blink. Left side of my face is always numb.

Question: What would you like people to know?

Answer: You should do your research before you get any procedure done. Don't just take the first doctor's advice. Please pray.

From All of Us

We all have God and prayer in our lives. I think that is what we want everyone to know.

Glorify the Lord with me; let us exalt his name together. (Psalm 34:3)

Chapter 9

The Book Continues

One good thing about writing a book is that there is always an option to delete or add to it. I deleted two chapters from the original manuscript, so I added two chapters. I wanted to make my book about two hours of reading. It wasn't difficult to find two chapters to write about. God wasn't through with me yet. He still had work for me to complete. I guess we all are works in progress.

I wrote at the end of Chapter 7, "I trust God to guide my path, to lead me through any storm that may come." I had no idea that, two years later, it would literally happen to me. I want to testify some more about God's glory.

August 12, 2016, I received a phone call from a friend. He asked me, "Is it flooding at your house?" He informed me that water was rising at his friend's house and sent me pictures on his cell phone. We only lived about fifteen minutes away from each other.

I hurried to my front door and looked out. It was raining, but I could clearly see the street. I could also see the grass in my front yard and in all my neighbor's yards. I explained to him that everything looked good at my house. That was the understatement of the year. I had only lived in the house for a year.

It rained all that day and night, and it didn't let up the next day. It was a day I will never forget, along with hundreds of others who lived in my town and the surrounding towns. I could see the water as it took over the street in front of my house. Its current went one direction and then flowed in the opposite direction. That's when I knew we were going to have a flood.

I walked to my neighbor's house and gave him my cell phone number, and he gave me his number. I told him to get ready and that we were going to have a flood. He explained to me that he had lived in his house for twelve years, and it had never flooded before.

Big spiders ran into our houses from our yards. They were trying to stay dry too. The water rose very quickly.

I should have left sooner. The water started rising so fast. It was a brown color, and you couldn't tell where the roads were. The water soon became too high for me to drive in. I was so scared. I made a place to stay in my attic. This was a bad decision and not a good idea! This is how people end up drowning in their houses. There is no way to get out of the attic, if the water continues to rise higher than the roof.

My sister-in-law phoned and begged me to call 911 so they would come rescue me. I did but was told that people in higher water would be rescued first.

I had a little teacup poodle. I didn't know what to do with her. I was scared that the people who rescued me wouldn't let me bring her. For some people that may sound ridiculous, but she is part of my family.

I was going to stay at my house but then saw a snake. Well that's all I needed to see. I am very, very scared of snakes. I threw my medicine, clothes, and dog food in a bag. I was crying and praying the whole time for God to please help me.

I covered my little dog with a blanket and explained to her

that the water was brown and she was also. If she jumped out of my arms, I wouldn't be able to see her and the current would take her away.

I walked out of my neighborhood in waist-high, brown, cold, stinky water. I used the mailboxes as markers so I would know where to walk. The current of the water was so strong it was very difficult to walk against. Objects brushed against my legs.

As I walked out of my neighborhood, people stood in the doorways of their flooded homes and stared at me. I think they were all in shock. When I walked out of that neighborhood, I left everything I owned behind, and it didn't bother me one bit. God helped me. He poured His biblical peace over me along with the raindrops.

Chapter 10

Blessings after the Flood

It took three days for the floodwaters to go down. On a Monday morning, I returned to my home to see what was left.

During the flood, everyone had gone into survival mode. I had prayed before, during, and after the flood, thanking God for keeping everyone, including myself, safe.

I hadn't grieved for my loss, but while I headed back to see the destruction that had been left behind, my stomach became upset. I could feel my body starting to shake as I approached my house. When I turned onto my street, I saw that my neighbor had a huge American flag waving her almighty proudness over the neighborhood. That flag gave me the much-needed courage and God gave me the much-needed strength to face my home.

As I walked into my house, it felt immediately different. An intruder had definitely entered my home. It appeared that eighteen to twenty-one inches of water was in my home. I discovered that it made no difference whether it was six or twenty-one inches of water. Its destruction was the same. You still had to replace four feet of Sheetrock. However, my vehicle had been spared.

I saw my neighbor outside. He asked, "Where do you start?" I answered, "One room at a time."

My preacher came by that afternoon. He looked inside my house and said, "Everything has to go."

I could not comprehend his words. I wondered, *Everything? What does he mean?*

He asked, "Do you have flood insurance?"

I told him, "No, I decided not to renew it."

He informed me that I would have to go take out a loan. He said that he and his teenage son would be back later that night to take off the baseboards. We stood in the middle of my living room as he prayed.

After the preacher left, I sat on my wet recliner. I didn't know what to do next. A thought came into my head, *Call your insurance company and ask when your flood insurance expired.*

I even questioned the thought, *What good would that do?*

My next thought was, *What do you have to lose?*

I pulled my cell phone out of my pocket and called my insurance company. The woman told me that my policy had expired on July 20. That day was August 15. I still don't know why these words came out of my mouth, but I asked, "Don't I have a thirty-day grace period?"

She said, "Yes."

I asked her, "If I pay my policy in full today, will I have flood insurance coverage?"

She hesitated and then asked me, "Are you going to make a claim?"

I said, "Oh yeah!"

She told me that she wanted to double-check with her supervisor before I paid all that money. She put me on hold, and I did the thank-you-God jig in the middle of my living room. She came back on the phone and explained that if I paid my flood insurance in full, my policy would not be interrupted, therefore, I would still have flood insurance coverage.

Do you see how God blessed me? If I had waited five more days to make that call, it would have been too late. God is so good!

I never complained even one time about what my insurance would or wouldn't pay. I was just so grateful. There were bad people who took advantage of flood victims, and the flood victims lost everything. They were such terrible creatures. I refuse to write about those people. I want my book to be about the blessings from God.

My son-in-law helped me cut and gut my house before he left for an out-of-state job. Every wall and the insulation behind the wall that was four feet high or lower had to be replaced. Every cabinet, door, and even the bathtubs had to be hauled out and put on the side of the road. All my furniture and appliances were piled there like the rest of the neighborhood's. My church family, my blood family, and my friends helped me move everything out of my house. My neighborhood looked like ground zero. We were all blessed that no lives had been lost.

Every day there were church members, friends, and even strangers who knocked at my door and gave me food, water, gift cards, and help. My nephew gave me get a dehumidifier from his work place to help dry out my house for about a week.

Franklin Graham's volunteer group called Samaritan Purse came and sprayed my house for mold. The most precious gift that they gave me was their prayers. Three men and I joined hands in my garage and prayed together, thanking God for his many blessings to me. All three of them were from different states and had come together in Lafayette, Louisiana, to serve in God's name. They came from Doylestown, Pennsylvania, Boone, North Carolina, and Kansas City, Missouri. They all signed a Bible, which they presented to me before they left. I will forever be grateful to them.

It was four months before I could move back into home. That

was faster than most people because, when my son-in-law came back home, he built cabinets for my house. My sister, brother-in-law, and friend opened up their homes to me while mine was being repaired. I enjoyed my time living with my friend and getting to know her family. I also had bonding time with my sister, which brought back childhood memories. We stayed up watching TV and eating popcorn.

I can't thank my mom and stepdad enough for all the hours that they helped me. Thank God for my church family. They let me borrow their truck and muscles to move me back home.

Before the flood, I hadn't even known the name of the neighbor who lived across the street. Now, not only do we know each other's names but check up on each other to see if help is needed. It's a shame that it took a flood to make this neighborhood develop closer relationships with one another. The neighborhood had gone through a stressful time, but we had all gotten through it.

Surviving a disaster brings out the love in us that God intended for us to share. I heard a knock on my door before Christmas. I opened it to find the neighborhood kids singing Christmas carols. It made my heart so happy to see this fellowship. One Sunday morning in church, three church members stood up and gave reports of the damage to their homes. They also thanked the church for all the help that they had received. I stood up and did the same but also professed my belief in Philippians 4:19, which says,

And, my God shall supply all your need according to His riches in glory by Christ Jesus.

My street with our house contents, ruined
and stacked on the roadside

Questions

Everyone should be able to answer these three questions. I will share my answers with you.

Question: Are you saved?

My answer: Absolutely yes!

Question: What will it cost you to get salvation?

My answer: It is free. Jesus paid the price for me or anyone who believes in Him and accepts Him into their life.

Question: Why were you saved?

My answer: To write this book and let everyone hear God's words.

My answers explain that Jesus Christ is the only answer. Please let Him help you!

He did promise that we would have trials and trouble in our lives, but He also promises to never leave or forsake us.

As I read in God's word daily, I kept coming to the same bible verse over and over.

"2 Corinthians 1:4" This contributed to me wanting to write this book.

God Bless   Monica Cayce

He comforts us in all our troubles so that we can comfort those in any trouble with the comfort we ourselves received from God. (2 Corinthians 1:4)

Monica Cayce 2016
My favorite Bible Verse is Psalm 46:10
Stand Still and Know that I Am God.
The one thing I would like people to remember
about me, is that I am a God fearing woman!
I believe all my suffering was designed for God's
purpose to display His Glory! Amen."